PRECIOUS GARUBA

God Through The Lens Of A Hardened Heart

Copyright © 2025 by Precious Garuba

All rights reserved. No part of this publication may be reproduced, stored or transmitted in any form or by any means, electronic, mechanical, photocopying, recording, scanning, or otherwise without written permission from the publisher. It is illegal to copy this book, post it to a website, or distribute it by any other means without permission.

First edition

This book was professionally typeset on Reedsy.
Find out more at reedsy.com

Contents

Introduction   1

I   Breaking the Ice

  1   Lost In the World   5
  2   Adjust   8

II   The Cry

  3   Relocated   13
  4   Faith Built In Silence   16
  5   Undoing   20
  6   Uncharted Territory   23
  7   Smoke Without Fire   26

III   THE CALL

  8   Deployed   33
  9   Interrupted Silence   37

IV   THE JOURNEY

  10   Magnifying Glass   43
  11   My Chosen Reality   46
  12   Restoring Identity   48

V	UNFORGIVENESS	
13	It Still Hurts	53
14	Body Memory	63
15	Chisel	66

VI	Relief	
16	Final Word	71
17	Journal Prompts	74

Introduction

Growing up, I thought I had it all figured out: finish school, attend university, secure a good job, get married by 25, have kids, watch them grow, and then retire. Live a not-so-perfect life, but a good enough one. And, of course, God would always be at the centre of it all. I never desired to be the model Christian, and I certainly wasn't. I had my fair share of misalignment, partied a little too hard, awakened love before its time, and lived through the consequences of my actions. But even in all that, I still believed there was a big man in the sky watching over me. Someone I needed to pray to and show up for on Sundays.

I was raised Pentecostal, living in Ireland. During the week, while at school, I was Catholic. I learned all about Mary, patron saints, and was taught how to pray with a rosary. On weekends, I was back in a traditional African Pentecostal church, learning about spiritual warfare, long-suffering, and how to serve God while oppressed, mixed in with church politics. So, I'd say my knowledge about God and religion, at least from a Christian standpoint, was quite broad. But in terms of actually knowing God and having a relationship with Him? That was more than foreign to me.

I

Breaking the Ice

1

Lost In the World

In 2015, I moved to the UK (London, to be specific) at a time when youth churches were on the rise. That came with all its complexities. We were 12 to 16-year-olds, unfamiliar with the idea of going to church without our parents. The hotspots of youth evangelism in my area, Peckham and Walworth Road, meant I could never walk through without being met by a group of young people asking, *"If you were to die tomorrow, where do you think you'd go?"* As a 12-year-old, of course, I would say, *"Heaven."* But the follow-up question would be, *"Have you given your life to Christ?"* I would hesitantly say no, and be met with a direct response: *"So you're going to hell."*

Now, as daunting as the word hell was back then, what felt even heavier was the question of giving my life to Christ, a name I had heard all my life. Jesus. Son of God. Christ. During my time in Sunday school, there was a Bible verse engraved in my memory:

Isaiah 9:6 — "For unto us a child is born, unto us a son is given, and the government shall rest upon his shoulder. And His name shall be called Wonderful Counsellor, Mighty God, Everlasting Father, Prince of Peace."

So I suppose you could say I knew of Christ. But despite growing up in church, I had never been asked such a question, and the idea of giving my life to Him felt like a decision I was too young and unprepared to make.

Yet I would still always say yes.

I gave my life to a man I didn't quite know, but had read a lot about, right there in the middle of the streets of Peckham. An invitation to their church would usually follow that moment. So, I started attending a church run by young people, whose zeal often came across as pretentious. Their smiles never seemed to fade from the beginning of the service until the end. To me, it felt like an act — one that everyone was in on but me.

I've always had this comparative nature, constantly measuring everything against what I already knew. So, when I found myself in this new, youth-centred version of church, one that spoke about modern-day problems but rarely offered real solutions, it felt jarring. It was nothing like the religious upbringing I had in Ireland. The teachings often contradicted the traditional Pentecostal values I'd been raised with, and that tension made it hard for me to fully settle. They touched on topics I sometimes felt too young to hear, which only opened me up to new levels of curiosity and confusion.

Over the years, I would go on to try six different churches, giving my life to Christ over and over again, each time still not fully knowing who He was but exposing myself to new teachings, varying interpretations, gifts of the spirt such as the prophetic, which as I understood it then, was this intense ability that someone could see my entire life from start to finish.

And deliverance, which I was petrified of. So much so that while others were praying to be delivered, I was quietly begging : "*If there are demons in me, just leave them therefore* ." Not because I didn't want to be free, but because I couldn't bear what felt like a humiliation ritual. The thought of being seen like that, undone in front of everyone, terrified me more than whatever it was I needed freedom from.

More often than not, I was left with more questions than answers. I became an expert church hopper, leaving at the slightest inconsistency with what I thought church should be.

2

Adjust

During all this, I was still a teenager, navigating challenges that often made me question where God was.

The move from Ireland to the UK wasn't something my parents discussed with me, so I never really had time to prepare. I just had to adjust. My home went from a two-parent household to a single-parent one. I was already the eldest of four siblings, but now there was a new weight of responsibility I had to step into without warning.

The shift from rural countryside living to a densely populated city was another major change. On top of that, I went from attending a Catholic all-girls school to a mixed public school that was, frankly, notoriously known in South East London. As you can imagine… there was a lot to adapt to.

There was friendship drama, boy drama, and emotional regulation issues (or, more honestly, anger issues). Some people have healthier outlets, but for me, there was no in-between; it was 0 to 100. I wasn't someone who talked about my feelings. I'd tried therapy a few times, but writing became my real outlet.

Talking to a stranger about how I felt or what was happening at home? That was a no-go. I'm Nigerian, and what happens at home stays at home.

Then, as life would have it, death made itself known. I began to lose family members to various illnesses, friends, and schoolmates to gang violence. And all these emotions I never let out had nowhere to go. I'll be honest, I didn't seek God through all of this. Neither did the people around me. But I did blame Him. Not always intentionally, but the fact that I didn't want to involve Him said enough. I didn't think I needed to. He could see everything, right? He knew what was happening and still chose not to step in.

Though despite all of that, I never stopped believing in Him.

When exam season came, I kept my streak of praying every day. On results day, the fear of failure and having to tell my parents meant I'd wake up early just to try and earn some extra points in heaven, hoping God would change the outcome.

When I had my first drunken experience, it was the bathroom floor of a shisha lounge that saw me crying and begging God to take it all away, promising I would never do it again. The days I'd come home late, smelling like every teenage movie stereotype, I'd instinctively motion the cross across my chest before walking in to greet my mother.

This was my life. It was all I had known, and eventually, I just accepted it. I don't know when, but my mentality had become "life is shit and you just have to get on with it"

I told you, I wasn't the model Christian.

As I said, it's not that I didn't believe in God. With everything going on, all the growing up and constant adjusting, I felt too in control of my own life to believe that He was looking out for me— it was easier to convince myself that He wasn't.

Gradually, it became routine to skip church. My family grew more relaxed. Unlike the strict environment I grew up in, where missing church wasn't even a question. We could now go months without praying, let alone stepping into a service.

It was just life.

II

The Cry

EXODUS 3:9
I have heard the cries of the people of Israel. I have seen the way the Egyptians have made life hard for them.

3

Relocated

Eventually, at university outside of London, I was fortunate enough to be placed with a flatmate whose very first question to me was, "Are you a Christian?" Now, I call her my destiny-helper, because without her, I honestly don't think I would have stepped foot in a church during my time at uni. I was completely immersed in the university lifestyle, often forgetting that I was there to study.

But she was adamant about finding a church while away from her home church. So, we began the search what I now call our month of "church shopping", and eventually we settled at an evangelical church with a youth service.

Surprisingly, it passed my internal "church checker", the quiet list of red flags I had built up over the years.

At the time, I didn't realise how lost and spiritually disconnected I'd become. I had built up so many walls towards church that I was just grateful to have a place where I could simply show up and try to reconnect with the faith I'd grown up with.

But, as always, God had other plans for me.

While attending this church, I began to realise the depth of the disadvantage that came with church hopping. I saw clearly that I had picked up bits and pieces from different churches, but never stayed long enough to build anything solid.

This time, the discomfort I felt wasn't like what I'd experienced in previous churches. It wasn't about the people or the place; it was internal. I had developed a deep insecurity about my spiritual maturity or, more accurately, my lack of it.

This insecurity made me feel unqualified to take part in things that, looking back now, I know would have helped me grow. But in the moment, I was too busy comparing myself to others. I'd watch the way people prayed, how they seemed to pour out scriptures effortlessly, how they flowed so freely in worship without the slightest trace of embarrassment.

Meanwhile, I had become known for my awkward little sidestep.

Then there were the people who had built real relationships with God. When asked, "What do you think God wants you to do?" they had answers. Real ones. The idea of God speaking to people felt strange to me. Yes, I knew God spoke— I'd heard about it, I'd read it. He spoke to Jeremiah, Moses, and Isaiah.

  He speaks to my pastor and other men and women of God.

But why hadn't He spoken to me?

RELOCATED

I knew I wasn't the model Christian, but surely, I'd done all the right steps.

I grew up in church. I'd read almost the entire Bible. I prayed. I tried.

Yet there was nothing. Not even a whisper.

This wasn't something I dwelled on for long, as it was easier to conclude that it didn't apply to me.

4

Faith Built In Silence

During my time at this church, I began to have experiences that I now recognise as encounters with the power of God. These moments started to shift my perception of Christianity and, in a way, led me to start asking the right questions. I say "ask" hesitantly. I had developed the idea that I was so far behind in my walk with God that there was no one I could ask any questions without the fear of being laughed at.

When the pastor would call a fast, I wouldn't know how long I was meant to fast for, so rather than ask, I just chose to go from the moment I woke up until midnight, eat one meal, and then start again. That might not seem like a problem to some, but I was so fragile in my relationship with God and with the church that if I slipped up like forgetting I was fasting or accidentally eating before the set time, I would call it quits.

I'd end the fast, pack my bags, and go back to London. That way, I didn't have to pretend everything was okay. This church community was great at checking in, so saying "I've gone back to London" became my go-to excuse to avoid further questions about church or my spiritual life.

I wish I could say I matured out of this quickly, but it went on for months, nearly a year. I didn't feel like my relationship with God was growing. I was still doing the same things I used to. Church was still just a Sunday thing, except now it included Bible study on Tuesday and a church community I was still trying to get used to.

I kept my usual circle of friends. People from different backgrounds, religions, and stages in life, which, to be honest, was more comforting than constantly feeling like I was at the bottom of the food chain at church. So, I think it's clear which direction I was heading in. Any chance to go back to London, I took. Any excuse to stay home and "bed-rot," I took. Being around people who didn't question my spiritual status? Even better.

Still, as per routine, I did my part and kept showing up to church. And eventually, I started to feel a little more comfortable. I could pray for longer without feeling like everyone was watching me.

One Sunday, while trying to rush out of church, having already booked my cab during the closing prayer, my pastor stopped me at the door and asked if I was coming to the night vigil. I wanted to say no. I know I said I could pray longer, but an entire night of prayer, surrounded by people who knew what they were doing? Not to mention the possibility of prophecy and deliverance? Yeah, that was a big no.

But for some reason, I didn't say no. And for an even bigger reason, I showed up two hours late, but I came. I should probably mention that by this time, I was in my second year of university and the infamous "uni depression" had caught up with me. I had been silently battling it for just over a year, and now, it was paired with a deeper frustration—a constant feeling that nothing would ever get better. I was overwhelmed all the time and found comfort in isolation and loneliness, hence the bed rotting. This opened the door to moments where life genuinely felt hopeless. I guess that's another reason why I kept going to church, and probably the real reason I went to that night vigil.

There wasn't much difference about this service, just extended prayer time and two guests: one a minister, the other a pastor. Or at least, that's what I thought.

The lights were dimmed, which made things a bit more comfortable for me. But then the man of God mounted the pulpit and asked for them to be turned on fully. He preached for a while, and then the power of God entered the room, and so did all my fear.

I can't count how many times I thought about leaving. Prophecy, deliverance… everything I didn't want was happening in that room, all at once. Though I guess the defeated mental state I was in was desperate enough to try anything for relief. I didn't even recognise the version of myself that sat there willing.

So, where I usually would've been praying for them to pass me by, this time I closed my eyes, and with all the intensity in me, I whispered, *"I'm ready, I'm not scared anymore."*

Almost immediately after I opened my eyes, the man of God looked directly at me and said, *"You,"* and signalled me to come forward.

I looked around, confused, then pointed to myself and repeated, *"Me?"* But before he could even respond, the ushers had already taken my glasses off and wrapped a cloth around me.

He didn't say anything. He just placed his hand on me, and I fell.

That was it.

This small, simple act was all I needed.

I never believed in "falling under the power." I always assumed people were pushed, or maybe just overwhelmed by emotion. Once, at a church I attended (church 3 of 6, if we're counting), the pastor climbed on the chairs and ran across them, laying hands and pushing people down as he went. That image had stayed with me, and it shaped my scepticism for a long time. But this moment was different.

I didn't feel forced, I didn't feel manipulated. It was involuntary and real.

And that tiny moment gave me a seed of faith: maybe there is more to God than I thought.

I told you my relationship with Him was fragile.

So, when the man of God made an altar call, I asked myself whether all those other times I had given my life to Christ, I had truly believed the way I do now.

The answer was a simple *no*.

So, I went forward. And this time, before the man of God could even reach me, I felt something stir. A heaviness. A deep, overwhelming intensity that couldn't be released by words.

And then I cried, but it wasn't just a cry. It was a bitter, heavy, from-the-depths-of-my-soul kind of cry. One that took everything out of me. One where, in the midst of it, it felt like I was finally telling God all the things I had been holding in for years.

I didn't fully understand it. But I needed it.

5

Undoing

From that day, that sound, that broken, unfiltered cry became my prayer language. As I was never good at talking about my feelings, that form of expression did something in me that words simply couldn't.

Of course, it was still difficult for me to just give up what I had so naturally done before. My prayers had always followed a routine: "Heavenly Father, I thank You, I worship You," and once all the formalities were done, I'd finally go in with my requests. But now, I couldn't even get a few words in without the intensity of tears building up inside me like that had become my new Amen. What used to be quiet time with God had now become a place where silence was completely absent, replaced instead with an overwhelming need to weep. And I don't use that word lightly. It wasn't a soft, graceful cry. It was an ugly cry— the kind that would make you feel embarrassed if anyone else saw you in that state.

But in the middle of the tears, the snot, and the audible sobs, I would decide to cry to God.

No words— and believe me, I tried to speak.

Just me and my brokenness, crying out to God to take care of battles I no longer had the strength to fight.

I can't say I particularly enjoyed doing it. It felt uncomfortable. It wasn't what I had been taught to do. I was used to bottling up my emotions so I wouldn't become a burden to anyone. Vulnerability scared me.

This was different.

It felt like what I needed to be doing, even if I didn't know whether God was listening. To be fair, I wasn't saying much, but still, I continued. A couple of weeks later, I was attending choir rehearsals. I had recently joined the choir and we had just come off a fast. As we were wrapping up, we spontaneously entered a moment of worship when my pastor walked in and said,
> "You don't have to come forward, but there's someone here... they don't talk to God. Their prayer language is tears."

From the very beginning of what he said, I believed he was talking about me, especially because he was aware of how I felt about the prophetic.

> "God is saying He hears your tears, and He wants you to know that He hears you."

I didn't say a word. I didn't move. I played it cool.

This might not seem like a profound moment to some, but for me, it changed everything.

That word altered the relationship I had with God. It stirred something in me—a desire for a real relationship with Him. So much so that when I went home, I typed into YouTube: "How do you pray?"

And I watched hours-long videos on prayer, on repeat.

From that day, worship songs began to feel different. My perspective began to shift.

God hears me.

God hears my tears.

He hears everything.

6

Uncharted Territory

I'd love to say that from then on, everything was perfect, a beautiful blend of tears, prayer, worship, and all the things I had been taught. Yes, things got better, but the process wasn't as seamless as I'd hoped.

I was now able to approach God in a new way that bridged the gap I had struggled with for so long. This new openness stirred in me a longing, sometimes even a desperation, for God to speak to me directly. Yet self-doubt kept me from reaching for Him fully. I felt I wasn't spiritual enough, consistent enough, or worthy enough.

But still, I prayed.
   Still, I went to church.

I was learning so much, experiencing so much. I was being exposed to different men of God, each teaching me something new, yet never contradicting one another. Looking back now, I realise that this was a pivotal season in my walk with God. I didn't know it then, but He was quietly undoing some of the red flags from previous churches, some I may have misunderstood, others were, in truth, teaching false doctrine.

My prayer life became the strongest it had ever been. I felt like I was finally maturing, finally becoming the Christian I had always thought I should be. I guess you could say I was on fire for God. I knew the prayer lingo, I was boldly speaking in tongues, I lifted my hands during worship, and I even stayed a little longer after service.

With all that growth, I found myself searching for results.
   My home life hadn't changed.
   My situation still felt heavy.

Life wasn't the perfectly happy place I thought I'd been promised. And that's when the real questions started to creep in, the kind most believers dread hearing, let alone thinking:

If God hears me, why hasn't He done anything?
   Why would He let me keep going through this?
   Why does it feel like He shows up for everyone else but me?
   If God can hear me, why would He allow all these bad things to happen?

I think that's a reality a lot of people are afraid to admit. We avoid questioning how life is going because we carry this idea that questioning life is the same as questioning God. And we've been taught we should just be grateful.

That's the belief I shared.

And because of it, I didn't know how to come before God anymore. Especially because of the revelation that He could hear me. So, when I prayed, I was no longer just releasing words—I was expecting an answer. But the more I waited, the more I feared I might be overstepping a boundary that, I now realise, never existed.

That fear made me pull away.

7

Smoke Without Fire

Pulling away wasn't just cutting down my hours at church; it was a quiet retreat that eventually led to me returning to London. For my final year at university, I stayed, and my excuse became, 'It's cheaper to commute.'

But deep down, I knew I was choosing to return to an unstable, yet familiar, church environment.

I'll be honest: I didn't see the issue at the time.

That's how I'd lived most of my life anyway — straddling the line between conviction and convenience.

Somehow, I convinced myself that all the maturing I had done, all the learning, had perfectly equipped me to handle life on my own.

I was "on fire," remember?

So, I went back to the life I knew, surrounded by people who didn't mention God beyond a casual "God forbid", allowing me to avoid the reality I wasn't ready to face. I was slowly slipping back into old patterns, this time dressed up as self-sufficiency.

And the scariest part?

No one around me questioned it.

Not even me.

Of course, now and then, I'd get a call or message from people from my university church encouraging me to keep building my relationship with God and to stay faithful. Random TikToks or Instagram posts would hit a little too close to home, but I ignored them. Sometimes I even blocked or unfollowed.

I was content with remaining oblivious.

As the months went by, I started to miss the routine of going to church, so I started church-shopping again in London, trying to find a place that would imitate the experience I had at my university church, somewhere that felt familiar, so I wouldn't have to start all over again.

But the search was completely unsuccessful.

One day, I received a call from my pastor. It wasn't long—he was just checking in. But then he asked a question I'd been avoiding:
"How's your relationship with God going?"
I answered, "It's... going."

He paused, then replied,

"I know. You're spiritually weak. Go and pray,"

and hung up.

I told you God spoke to him.

Although it was abrupt, and at the time, it almost felt cold. But looking back, it was symbolic, like He was forcing me to confront the very silence I had been avoiding. The silence had become the backdrop of my prayer life. The truth is, despite everything I'd learned, it felt like I had hit erase the moment I moved. I had left the only place where I truly felt like God was. I hadn't realised it before, but I had tied my entire relationship with God to that church at university. Outside of it, nothing felt good enough. I tried recreating what I had there, listening to the same worship songs, reading over old Bible study notes, but nothing worked. I didn't even cry during my quiet time any more. I felt numb.

And I wanted to give up.
   I really did.
   It felt so much easier to just live the way I had before. The world was more straightforward, more predictable.

The painful part was… I didn't want that life anymore.

And that frustration started to boil inside me.

I wanted the relationship back. I wanted to feel God again. So, instead of trying to repeat the same tired routines of prayer, I just sat there—in silence—and asked, "God… what do You want from me?"
   I told Him I was tired. Completely exhausted.

And no, I'm not going to pretend He responded with a booming voice. If He did speak, I didn't hear Him. So, I got on with my day. I had plans to go out, but because of that heaviness in my spirit, I decided to walk to the station instead of taking the bus. I kept the conversation going as I moved from rambling thoughts, frustration, silence, and even distraction.

Then, mid-thought, I suddenly remembered a moment during one of our night vigils. A man of God had taught from Isaiah 6, specifically the moment when Isaiah encountered the Lord and heard Him ask, "Whom shall I send?" The teaching was heavy. By the end, the man of God made a call to those who felt the weight of the message. He invited them to the front. I didn't go up, but I was burdened deeply.

As he led them in prayer, he cried out with fire:
  "Wherever you go, let yokes be broken.
  Wherever you go, let people be set free.
  Wherever you go, wherever the Lord sends you, may you go with power.
  You will go with authority.
  You will go with the might of God.
  You will go with the symbol of God.
  You will go, and you will not look back."

Despite not joining them at the front, I stayed quietly at the back, whispering my response.

And as the room pressed deeper into prayer, I found myself saying
  "Send me. Send me."

It wasn't something I had planned to say. I didn't overthink it. It just came out instinctively. Almost like my spirit knew before my mind caught up.

That memory hit me hard.

I looked at my life—where I was now—and it was nothing like the girl who had said "Send me." My choices had brought me far from where I thought I would be. And in that moment, the tears returned.

But this time, they weren't just out of frustration.

It was tears of repentance.

I wasn't crying over unanswered prayers or unmet expectations; I was crying because I realised how long I had been carrying things I never spoke about. I was crying to God to forgive me... because I didn't know what to do anymore. This wasn't a moment I fully understood, but in that moment, I knew I was tired of doing it all on my own.

Yes, life didn't look the way I had hoped. But if I'm being honest, I wasn't doing anything to change that.

I'd grown accustomed to incomplete progress, stuck in a cycle that felt familiar, maybe even safe. A cycle where I'd start strong, drift off, and bow out quietly whenever real change required more from me. I always knew my exit points. I preferred temporary solutions, ones that gave the illusion of movement without going anywhere.

But this time was different.

This time, I didn't have the option to retreat.

I couldn't run back to university. That season had ended. If I were going to move forward, I had to be intentional. I had to rebuild this relationship with God, not in the context of comfort, but during unfamiliarity.

I couldn't be picky anymore.

III

THE CALL

EXODUS 3:16
Go and gather the elders and tell them this: the lord God of your ancestors, has appeared to me. The God of Abraham, Isaac and Jacob spoke to me. He says: I care about you, and I have seen what has happened to you in Egypt

8

Deployed

Later that week, my mum invited me to visit the new family church they'd been attending while I was away. It was a new church, still small, with plenty of room for growth and no place to hide.

At the end of the service, I was introduced to the First Lady of the church. It began as a warm, friendly conversation until it took a sharp turn. She asked me if I could sing, and before I could even open my mouth, my mum immediately answered, "Yes." And just like that, I was no longer a visitor; I was the newest member of the choir.

Not just any choir member, either. She looked at me and said, "You'll be leading worship next Sunday."

Me. The same girl who had been running from church.

Me. Who hadn't prayed properly in months.

I left that service in shock. The very next Tuesday, I found myself back at my university church, an unplanned visit, what felt like an emergency meeting with my pastor. The man who hears from God.

I was hoping he'd give me an out.

Something—anything—that would get me off the hook.

I didn't feel ready. I didn't feel qualified. And deep down, I think I was afraid that stepping into this role meant I'd have to face everything I'd been avoiding for so long.

And that is exactly what happened.

He didn't tell me "No."

He didn't rescue me with an easy way out.

Instead, he encouraged me.

Not exactly what I had travelled two hours to hear, but looking back, it was exactly what I needed.

Like I said, it was a small, new church. And while that meant there was a lot of room for growth, it also meant there was *a lot* of room for error.
   From me.
   From the one-man sound team.
   From our four, occasionally five-person choir.
   From the congregation that sometimes didn't even show up.

It was honestly one of the most demotivating environments I'd ever been in.

Of course, I wanted to leave. I had threatened to at least ten times.

This wasn't what I thought "being sent" looked like.

I think what kept me going was that prayer.

"Send me."

That was the thing that held me accountable.

At first, I found myself constantly comparing everything to my university church. That had been my standard, my measure of what church should look and feel like. But God slowly shifted my perspective.

It wasn't the *goal*.
It was the *blueprint*.
It was almost like an experience that I had, so I could bring that *hope* into places like this.
Places that didn't yet look like the vision I had seen, but could.

That shift didn't happen overnight. I often felt isolated.

Frustrated, too, especially when things didn't go well.
When the sound cut out.
When the choir hadn't learned the song.
When the room felt empty, and I had no idea how to lead people who weren't even showing up.

I couldn't keep riding that emotional roller coaster. It was draining.

So, I brought it to God.

I started praying not just for myself, but for the choir, for the church, for the people I was serving with.

I didn't always see immediate changes around me.

But something began to shift *within* me.
I had more patience.

More peace.

More compassion for the people I once wanted to give up on.

I started learning about other departments, asking how I could help, especially with sound.

In doing so, I realised I was starting to see God as *my partner*, not just someone I reported to.

And as that relationship changed, I started to notice something else.

I began to feel like God *did* speak to me, just not always in the ways I had expected.

Not through someone else.

Not through a voice from heaven.

But through *thoughts*.

Quiet impressions.

Subtle nudges.

It reminded me of something I'd once seen on TikTok—before I'd unfollowed every Christian content creator in frustration.

She said:

"Imagine if someone always came to you for help, but never stayed long enough to hear the advice."

At the time, I didn't think it applied to me.

But now, I couldn't shake it.

It stayed with me.

Because deep down, I knew I had been doing exactly that.

9

Interrupted Silence

It wasn't an instant fix.
 To be honest, I had a lot of unlearning to do.

The silence was uncomfortable.

I thought that if I just waited a little longer, everything would change, that the voice of God would suddenly fill the room when I prayed, that He would start handing me the next steps, clearly and directly. But that couldn't have been further from the truth.

Don't get me wrong—I *tried*.

There were moments I'd say "Amen" and just sit there, waiting. Waiting for something. Anything. Even just a slight sound or a sense of presence.

But most times, I got distracted.
 By memories.
 By random song lyrics.
 By old, embarrassing moments I'd rather not relive.

Sometimes I gave up. Other times, I'd even make up a response in my head, just to break the silence.

But I kept going.
  I didn't stop praying.
  I just started praying *differently*.
  At the end of each prayer, I began asking God to give me a scripture.

The first time, I thought I heard: *James 14:22*
  And of course, to my surprise, there is no *James 14:22*

But I held on to the fact that I'd heard "James."
  So, I read the whole thing.
  And by the time I got to James 1:2 — *"Consider it pure joy, my brothers and sisters, whenever you face trials of many kinds..."*
  I knew I was supposed to be reading James.

The next time I prayed, I heard James 14:22 again and again. At some point, it's only right that I question if I was truly hearing God, but I think the desperation to hear from Him allowed me to keep pushing.

I was looking for anything, so much so that I made my rule of thumb,
  When in doubt, read it all.

Until eventually, I heard another word.

Exodus.

No chapter. No verse. Just: **Exodus.**

Of course, as always, I questioned, Was it from God? Or just a random thought I created to fill the silence again?

But somehow, deep down, I *knew*.

Because nothing about that moment would have led me to think of *Exodus*.
   It didn't make sense to me.

And *that* was exactly why I knew it wasn't from me.

Amidst all of this, I felt a quiet, persistent pull to obey.
   To read.
   To listen.
   To trust.
   So, I did.

IV

THE JOURNEY

EXODUS 14:31
When the people of Israel saw the great power, but the Lord had used against Egyptians, they fear the Lord and they trusted the Lord and his servant Moses.

10

Magnifying Glass

It wasn't a book I was unfamiliar with. *Exodus* had always been used to explain how God answers the cries of the oppressed. This was where God revealed Himself through a burning bush—yet even then, Moses wrestled with insecurity, questioning whether he was truly worthy to be Israel's deliverer.

It holds the infamous parting of the Red Sea and has inspired countless "covenant-keeping God" songs.

But despite all that, while reading it this time, it felt like the first time. I'm not sure if it was because of the reason I was reading it, you know, the whole "Exodus" of it all, or because I was intentionally reading, looking for the reason *why* I was reading.

It took me about a week to finish it. And because I'm a visual learner, it was naturally followed by a Netflix watch of *Testament: The Story of Moses*.

I want to say that reading it left me confused, that it didn't make any sense why God would want me to read it, or that it didn't relate to me. In reality, the book spoke to me in words, in moments, in ways I couldn't have imagined.

It wasn't just about God delivering the Israelites and them still longing to return to slavery. It wasn't just about Moses being raised as a deliverer, standing as a representative of God before Pharaoh. It wasn't just about Pharaoh's stubbornness that persisted right to the very end.

Yes, all of that was important. But what stuck out to me most was how God showed up *differently* to each person. He didn't look the same to everyone, and yet, He was still God.

To Moses, God was his friend. He had that tangible, physical encounter with Him, and He never left him. God didn't just equip him; He encouraged him, defended him even against his family. He made His relationship with Moses evident to all who encountered him, and He provided, although Moses' character flaws didn't always meet His standard.

To the Israelites, God was the great and mighty One. Many might call Him their saviour, but what I saw was a relationship that lacked intimacy, a relationship where the closeness that could've been gained was met with resistance. Despite God saving them with powerful miracles to free them from oppression, when things got tough, they couldn't recognise His hand at work. Even though they knew the great land ahead of them was a promise from God they'd held onto for 430 years, and despite witnessing the impossible that God did for them, when He tried to encounter them the way they perceived Him to be, they rejected Him.

To Pharaoh, God was just that—God—but through the lens of a hardened heart. God showed up as everything Pharaoh knew Him to be. When He told Moses, **"You will be like a god to Pharaoh,"** it revealed His intentions from the beginning. This was only further solidified when Pharaoh's magicians were able to replicate the same signs and wonders. But then God said He would harden Pharaoh's heart.

I always wondered why God would do that when things could have happened more quickly and smoothly. But now, I realise that He did it for me, for the Israelites, for Moses, and you.

God did it all to show that He can reveal Himself in many ways. But when our hearts are hardened, we struggle to accept the fullness of who He is, we reduce Him to what we know and what we want Him to be. We cling to our understanding, resisting the mystery of His nature. A hardened heart makes it hard to relinquish control. It makes it hard to trust Him. And without trust, without surrender, we cannot build depth in our relationship with Him.

11

My Chosen Reality

I didn't fully grasp it at first. To be honest, I ran with my desire. Even though a mirror was being held up, showing me how I viewed God, I chose to focus on building the kind of relationship I imagined, like the one between God and Moses. I wanted to become a friend of God. I knew it was something He would want too, so I started creating a daily routine: set times for prayer, Bible study, worship, and even space to cry if I needed to. I thought this would make me a better Christian, a better friend, and eventually, God's friend. But that rhythm only lasted about two weeks. When I couldn't keep up, I'd beat myself up, then try again or sometimes not at all.

This time, though, felt different from all the times before. I was determined to find something that worked. Something that worked for me. Something I genuinely enjoyed doing. Looking to Moses as a blueprint had its benefits; it kept me reflecting on what I had read. I began to consider what Moses was doing before God encountered him. And I saw it: he was a shepherd.

I had no intention of becoming a shepherd, but there were a few things I genuinely enjoyed. I sing, I write songs, and I journal. These were just hobbies, things I never really took seriously. But there was a quiet determination in me that kept pushing. So, I started to worship more, singing to God throughout my day. It came naturally, and given that I was also the worship leader, I was singing all the time. And it was a lot.

Eventually, I realised I needed something more sustainable, something that didn't rely on my voice. That's when I began journaling to God.

I'll be honest, it was hard at first. I had no idea what to say. I'd often begin with "Dear God" and end up writing out my prayers. It wasn't a problem, but it didn't feel like a journal; it felt more like a prayer book. What I needed was something that felt like a conversation, something that felt like talking to a friend.

So, I started telling God everything, day by day, moment by moment. Sometimes I'd forget, of course, life happens.

I'm not even sure how to describe the relationship that began to form between us. I had grown comfortable with our previous dynamic, God as my partner. But looking back, I realise that version of partnership had become an invisible wall. I wasn't lying to God, not exactly, but I was only bringing Him the things I thought I could handle. I'd tell Him about my struggles, but I wasn't surrendering them.

And the irony of it all? "Surrender" had become one of my go-to words in worship. I sang it often. I even led others to sing *"Withholding Nothing by William McDowell."* But I wasn't doing it. When I didn't have much to say, I'd just use the journal like a notebook. Jotting down quick thoughts or new songs I thought about for Sunday, I just kept showing up and writing. I guess it became my way of practically doing life with God.

12

Restoring Identity

During all of this, life started to change quickly. I had just finished university, which came with this heavy anxiety around all the transitions I couldn't control. I was also nannying part-time, something I hadn't planned to do long-term, so I ended up quitting. I started making some decisions simply because I felt led to, even though I didn't fully understand what that meant at the time.

I was still attending my family church, but I started experiencing resistance. Building my relationship with God also meant I was maturing spiritually, a lot quicker than I expected. It was like everything I'd ever learnt over the years was suddenly coming together and making sense, but in a way that was deeply personal to me.

No one prepares you for what it's like to mature in Christ — how discovering your identity in Him doesn't always make people happy for you. Especially when those people saw you at your weakest. Trying to step back into alignment with God wasn't exactly met with open arms, and that's me putting it nicely.

All this maturing and change started to show up in my friendships and relationships, too. I had prayed the dangerous prayer, "God, if this person isn't supposed to be in my life, remove them." A prayer I never thought I'd say, but sure enough… they did start to leave like flies.

There's this idea that spiritual things stay spiritual, but when they start manifesting in real life, it can hurt. Suddenly, I found myself back in what felt like isolation. But this time, it wasn't voluntary. This time, I wasn't the one calling the shots. My life felt like it was being led by someone else, and honestly, I struggled with that.

I knew I wanted a life with God, one where I could trust Him completely, and everything in my life would align perfectly. But what I didn't anticipate was the unlearning and healing I'd have to go through. That whole "it's just life" mindset was far from what God intended for me, and He wanted to deal with it from the root.

V

UNFORGIVENESS

13

It Still Hurts

Sunday 9th Febuary 2025 3:16am

I came here to tell you how I have been feeling for the last few days. You led me to read my last entry about my feelings. It just reminded me of why I am going through things. I've noticed that I am low key prophesying into my own life without knowing it. When I come here, I just write literally what comes to mind. It's my best effort at just surrendering everything circling my mind before it consumes me. I had written how I feel concerning the season I was in, which is about trusting You and how it would be a struggle for me. Now, here I am, ten days later, about to tell you how hard the last few days have been, and You have been telling me to trust and be patient. But I am just now coming to terms with that. I keep praying for wisdom, and yet I am now just realising that I have gotten it, but I didn't recognise it.

You've called me into a knowing of times and seasons concerning myself and, at times, those around me. That is so ahead of my scale of thinking that I just now realise I need to pray about it. Spiritually, I have matured so much, but I guess this would be one of the disadvantages of being carnal-minded. I've tried to have a spiritual approach with a carnal view. I am spiritually minded, but I have to acknowledge that with You speeding me up, I have to personally slow down and shift my perspective.

And as You call me into that depth of understanding, the do's and the don'ts, the why's and the why not's. When You said it's not a battle of flesh and blood, but that of the spirit, You weren't just talking about the enemy, but our spirit man versus the flesh, especially the mind. You made me know for years that my own self-thinking is a huge weakness for me. I know it's something You've delivered me from, but I've come to learn that even my own expectation of deliverance has been wrong. Things don't just stop. First, it needs to be identified, and then, in partnership with the Holy Spirit, things are put into place to turn things around. This is my deliverance. I want the change. I just had to understand why. The past few days, I've really had to lean into that whole 'remain-teachable' mentality. I don't have it all figured out. Family and society really, made me believed that I did, but then, inherently, I just believed that I was in control, and, essentially, I idolised myself. I implemented my own doctrines, belief systems, rules and regulations, reward systems. I actually tried to replace You with myself. So that brings me to today. I've been saying I surrender, I've been saying I trust You, but, in reality, I haven't, and I don't, but I want to.

I don't know what genuine surrender looks like.
I don't know what genuine trust looks like.

I don't know what genuine, pure love looks like.

Remaining teachable, I guess, means stepping away from/letting go of things that you thought you understood, unless you wouldn't be in this place of learning if what you knew was right. Teachers don't go to school to learn, only mature. I have to stop and step out of my own ways because right now, I'm getting in my own way.

What brought me to this point and why am I struggling to let go? I constantly ask You to search me where pride has creeped in, areas of my heart that are not in alignment. I haven't asked You to search me for areas of my heart that are still hurting.

Honestly, I can name a few, and I guess this will be the start of that deliverance. Holy spirit help me........

1. What's heavy on my heart today - Church hurt. It's been years since I've allowed church to be the source of pain. In my early years, I first experienced this when my parents left Bethel and noticed how various relationship breakdowns caused this. This hurt was me just being collateral damage. Going to Amazing Grace just made me lose interest in religion and relationship. The dynamics just changed. Getting older, now in the UK, the exposure to youth ministries was overwhelming and toxic. I gave them a few goes, but the disappointment every time, due to leadership and members. Filler years where I rekindled with you in uni during my darkest years, to then returning home and having to navigate that season, led me to

The Out Pouring Glory Ministry, (the family church). Now, one year later, with the leadership and my family dynamic has pushed me back into church hurt. I know it's having an effect on me because I'm ready to run again.

2. I'll keep this one honest and brief Relationship. I haven't healed from any of the hurt of either romantic or platonic relationships. 2022 and 2023 the breakdown of all of those relationships... It really affected me, but I have honestly just suppressed them. Amin, I know it's for my own good, but it definitely still hurts. Saul still confuses me to till this day, and yeah, the rejection hurts. Teddy. Hurt. For my own good, but I believe the desire for close female relationships is what is fueling that hurt. Betrayal is what is channelling the hurt for Oyin and Bela. And, surprisingly,

the original catalyst of platonic friendship breakdowns, Amira. Now, this is me being so raw and real damn. Secondary school was really an experience.

3. Father daughter relationship. Now, this hurt is one that I believe now I'm just suppressing. I have forgiven my dad, but to say the hurt has left is not accurate. I feel like I don't let him in, leaving him to just observe me rather than know me. I've said it time and time again, I know it has now had an effect on my relationship with You. I want to have a relationship with You deeper than a father-daughter one, or more than my tainted perception of one. I call You Abba because this is my perception of You and my expectation. If my view of a father is tainted and toxic, then I will naturally

treat this relationship how I treat the one with my dad. I wanted You to fix me and that view, but I didn't relinquish control. I wanted You, Abba, to fit into a box. I wanted You to observe me and then find Your place or squeeze Yourself into my life. Don't make too many changes, just be here when I need you and fill the abandonment issues up. I'll weaponise You, almost like, 'Don't let me go and get my dad.' Funny, but not funny.

I've now realised more than anything, Abba, I've needed a friend. You knew that. When You first revealed Your voice to me, one of the first things You said was, 'Do not worry about the friends, I will take care of that.' The second time You spoke, so clearly, You called me your friend. 'Precious, my friend, I know you.'
That brings me to my next hurt,

4. friendship hurt.
This has caused the prominent feeling of loneliness in my life. I have people who called me their friend and then betrayed me. I am sure I have hurt others, but the level of hurt and impact this has had on me really shaped me. So much so, that till this very day, I still struggle with this. And not letting people close is the only boundary I know how to maintain.

My arm is hurting now, Abba, so I'm going to end here. I pray You see me here and help me. Help heal me in the best way I know that You will. Teach me genuine friendship. Heal the brokenness and bitterness in my heart. Let me learn and experience genuine friendship. Love Your daughter who is trying to be Your friend.

14

Body Memory

I know that's a lot to unpack, and to be honest, at first I didn't even want to share this part of my journey. But this is my "why."

There's something about writing down your pain, making it tangible instead of carrying it silently, that allows you to finally see its weight. I was in a season where God had called me away from so much in my life, and I didn't understand why. I was being obedient to where He was leading me, but it truly felt like the wilderness. I believed in God Almighty, so I knew I would end up somewhere good, but the journey required me to go through tests of endurance. These tests were designed to expose what was going on inside me that God wanted me to release.

When I sat down to write that journal entry, I will be honest, I came from a place of frustration. I could see the option to go back to how things were when I was in control. I was going through so much at the time, especially within the church, that the resistance I was facing felt like something I could blame on God. I thought my obedience to Him was the cause of my suffering, not realising that people's choices to treat me poorly were their choices to make.

What I had written ten days earlier was this: "I'm following You, I'm doing things Your way, I'm serving, I'm praying, I'm doing everything right… so why does it feel like things are getting worse?" That blame was the reason why it had been ten days since my last entry.

Ten days may not sound long, but for someone who had been talking to God every day, it was too long. It revealed the true nature of my heart. I said I trusted Him, but I didn't, especially not then. I said I had surrendered, but I was already running. I said I loved Him, but I was hurting so much that I felt I had no love to give.

And that was why God had me in that season. At the time, I wanted Him to just tell me why I was going through all of this. Why did I have to face so much? But the truth is, I was a little stubborn. I truly believed I had life figured out, and that self-reliance had not developed overnight.

Once I admitted where I truly stood with God, I realised I was not there just to vent. I did not want to continue the way I was going. I wanted to let it out and let it go. That understanding is what brings true deliverance. The honesty removes the wool from over your eyes so you can break the cycle.

The truth was, I didn't feel like I was still dealing with the trauma from those situations, along with many others I could have written down if my arm hadn't grown tired. I had held onto it for so long that it had become part of me. It had started to lead me.

I was being led by trauma.
   By anxiety.
   By depression.
   By loneliness.
   By rejection.
   By bitterness.
   By abandonment issues.
   By hopelessness.

By shame.
By grief.
By trust issues.
By unforgiveness.
By doubt.
By a lack of confidence.
By feelings of unworthiness.
By comparison.
By heartbreak.
By jealousy.

They influenced how I prayed, how I loved, how I protected myself, and how I saw God. My heart had hardened in so many ways, and if I had continued like that, the list would have only grown longer and my resistance towards God stronger.

That's why God took Israel the long way instead of leading them straight into the Promised Land. He saw what their time in Egypt had done to them—how it had built a dependence on the life they had known before, especially in times of trouble. He saw that they still carried idols in their hearts, but most importantly, they still carried one fixed perception of Him: the God they cried out to only in distress. And so that was how they continued to see Him.

God wanted to break that cycle. He wanted them to reach a place where they would never have to return to that kind of bondage again. And that is exactly what He was doing with me.

15

Chisel

I didn't see it then, but this was the start of a healing journey, one where all the fruits left behind from these situations needed to be broken and let go of. All the unforgiveness had run its course, and I had to repent and break the bondage.

I had to step away from things where I found my identity, like work, certain friendships, and my role as worship leader. Leading worship may have been premature, but it taught me a lot about myself. It also showed me the standard not just the church required of me, but the one God did. Worship is truly a lifestyle, not just a moment on the altar, and I really need to die to self in order to sustain it.

One thing I wasn't prepared for was that the pursuit of being God's friend would first require me to learn how to be His daughter. I felt that would be the biggest struggle for me, because I needed to understand Him as Father. Yet, the pursuit of that relationship led me directly to His Son, Jesus.

So, like twelve-year-old Precious, I made a decision, one I now felt old enough and prepared to make. This time, I was giving Him my yes, not out of fear or in comparison to the many times I had done so before. I was saying yes to Him truly with my heart and not just with my mouth. I was deciding to follow Jesus, because He is the only one who can lead me to my Father, transform my hardened heart, and the way I had been seeing life.

VI

Relief

"Then Jesus said, "Come to me, all of you who are weary and carry heavy burdens, and I will give you rest. Take my yoke upon you. Let me teach you, because I am humble and gentle at heart, and you will find rest for your souls. For my yoke is easy to bear, and the burden I give you is light.""
Matthew 11:28-30

16

Final Word

My journey with God is far from over. And I'm truly grateful for everything I went through. It didn't break me. I came through it.

I'm filled with hope that my story encourages someone to keep going. If any part of you relates to my journey, even in the smallest way, this is your sign that God still loves you and is deeply interested in you.

Just as He inspired every book in the Bible with us in mind, He also calls believers to share their journeys with you in mind.

So, with that same heart, I leave you with this prayer.
   I pray that this book draws you into real, honest, and truthful communion with God, where He begins a deep healing in you, restoring you to the very person He created you to be.

I pray that every word spoken over you, by others or by yourself, that does not align with His truth is undone in the name of Jesus.

I pray that any coping mechanisms you've developed just to survive are broken off you by the power of the Holy Spirit.

The Bible tells us that only God is the righteous judge. So I pray that any judgements you've spoken over yourself, or that others have spoken and you've come into agreement with, are cancelled in Jesus name.

I pray for supernatural healing so complete that those around you will not recognise the person you become.

I pray that the fruit of the Spirit—love, joy, peace, patience, kindness, goodness, faithfulness, gentleness and self-control, will begin to manifest in every area of your life.

I pray for a divine restoration to your mental health, in Jesus' name.

I pray that God places heaven-appointed pastors and mentors in your life who will support and uplift you throughout your journey.

I pray that anyone you open up to about your story will meet you with compassion, understanding and the grace to walk alongside you.

I pray you will recognise the love of God in your life in a deep and unshakeable way, and come into the full assurance that He will never leave nor forsake you, even when it doesn't feel like it.

I pray that you will be surrounded by a godly community and that every cycle of isolation and self-inflicted loneliness is broken.

I pray that you will love yourself the way Christ loves the Church, sacrificially and without shame.

I pray that you forgive yourself as freely as God the Father has forgiven you.

And finally, I pray that any voice trying to drag you back into condemnation is silenced in the name of Jesus.

FINAL WORD

Amen.

17

Journal Prompts

JOURNAL PROMPTS

Date:

1. What would you say is the current status of your relationship with God?
   *Meditate on Isaiah 29:13 before answering.

2. Do you feel like you know God on a personal level, or do you know of Him?
   *Meditate on Matthew 7:21-23 before answering.

3. Tell God about your day-to-day life.
   *Meditate on Psalm 62:8 before answering

4. Tell God about a situation that tends to occupy your mind throughout the day — something from the past that often circles in your thoughts.
   *Meditate on 1 Peter 5:7 before answering

5. Tell God about times you wish He showed up to help you.
   *Meditate on Job 13:3 before answering.

Note:
If you feel stuck on how to answer ask the Holy Spirit to help you and by faith pick up your pen and begin to write.

Date:

JOURNAL PROMPTS

Date:

Date:

JOURNAL PROMPTS

Date:

Date:

JOURNAL PROMPTS

Date:

Date:

JOURNAL PROMPTS

Date:

Date:

JOURNAL PROMPTS

Date:

Printed in Dunstable, United Kingdom